Bailey & Canteen Theme

They ride across the prairie wide,
They're always side by side,
From dawn till setting sun.
You won't see one without the other,
They're closer than brothers,
Bailey and Canteen.

Chorus:
Best friends (best friends),
Bailey and Canteen,
Best friends (best friends)—
They're brown as a berry from ridin' the prairie.
All day long, they sing this song:
"We're joined by the heart, never apart, best friends."

Bridge:
You'll never see Canteen without Bailey by his side;
They started out together and partnered up for life.
Like birds of a feather, they stick together,
Bailey and Canteen.

Except as noted below, all sound tracks and vocals recorded and mixed by Aaron Minick at The Play Room Studio, Smyrna, TN. Mastered by Marty Shrabel at AHA Productions, Goodlettsville, TN. Audio tracks for "Bailey & Canteen Theme" and "Good Night, Canteen" recorded and engineered by Mike McIntyre at Wright Studio, Nashville, TN.

Eddy Bolton: Series writer and creator; co-producer of audio tracks and story narrator.
Johnny Minick: Co-producer of audio tracks; voice for introduction.
Aaron Minick: Co-producer of audio tracks; arranged sound effects and background music; audio engineer for vocals.
Mikchael Demus: Audio engineer for music tracks.
Gus Gaches: Co-producer of audio tracks for "Bailey & Canteen Theme" and "Good Night, Canteen."

Musicians
Harold Bradley: Lead and rhythm guitar. Billy Linneman: Upright bass. Aaron Minick: Drums, percussion, and keyboard. Johnny Minick: Accordion and piano. Bruce Watkins: Fiddle, mandolin, lead and rhythm guitar, and upright bass. Jason Webb: Piano, strings, and keyboard.

Vocalists
Voice of Bailey: Julie Bolton. "Bailey & Canteen Theme" vocals: Eddy Bolton, Aaron Minick, and Johnny Minick. "Bailey & Canteen Theme" children's background vocals: Megan Cannon, Rachel Elrod, Kylie Gaches, Briana Sparks, Megan Watson, Brooke Welch, and Jordan Welch. "Good Night, Canteen" background vocals: Eddy Bolton, Rod Curtis, Gus Gaches, and Louie Wilson. "Angels Are Always Around Us" children's background vocals: Sherry Minick, Amanda Williams, Karen Williams, and Lyndsey Williams.

Special thanks to Sandy Brazile and The Bailey Hat Company, Fort Worth, Texas.
Eddy Bolton is an endorsed artist for Greg Bennett Guitars.

ISBN 0-7847-1824-5

12 11 10 09 08 07 06   9 8 7 6 5 4 3 2 1

Canyon Rescue!

STORY & SONGS BY **EDDY BOLTON**

ILLUSTRATED BY **JERRY PITTENGER**

Standard® PUBLISHING

Bringing The Word to Life

Cincinnati, Ohio

This is a story 'bout a cowboy named Bailey
And his pony that he called Canteen.
They rode the range together in all kinds of weather,
And through the years became best friends, you see.

They were going to Switchback Canyon tomorrow,
But they camped 'neath the starry sky tonight.
Frogs were croaking, crickets were chirping,
And there were strange-looking shadows in the moonlight.

Bailey snuggled up to Canteen to use his neck for a pillow,
And his big body kept him toasty and warm.
And Bailey was nary a bit scared, while he was lying there,
'Cause he knew Canteen would keep him from harm.

Canteen rose at sunup to the smell of flapjacks cooking,
And he munched down a fair bit of hay.

Bailey tossed the saddle on Canteen's back,
Mounted up, and they trotted away.

They combed their hair by the river,
brushed their teeth with a shiver,
In water so cold they turned blue.

And when they stood just right, with the sun for a light,
Why, they could use the river as their mirror too.

The sun was high in the sky, Canteen was steppin' with pride
As he inched down the trail on the canyon wall.
Now that ol' Switchback was steep—Bailey sat deep
As he prayed, "Lord, I hope we don't fall!"

The prayer had just cleared his lips when ol' Canteen tripped;
Then his hooves just sorta froze on the trail.
Bailey lost his grip, from the saddle he slipped,
And down into the canyon he fell.

He clung to an old snag that had broken his fall—
Though he tried, he couldn't reach Canteen's tail.
But God had sent an angel when Bailey first prayed,
And he said, "Don't worry, God sent me to help."

The angel said, "Canteen,
   throw your rope to your friend.
Hold on tight with your teeth and then—

Just pull Bailey up till he reaches the trail,
And we'll all be together again."

"Whew! That was a close call!" said Bailey,
As he thanked God for saving him today.

He said, "I knew God sent angels to guard us,
And I'm really glad he sent you our way!"

Round up all these Bailey & Canteen adventures!

0-7847-1824-5

0-7847-1825-3

0-7847-1826-1

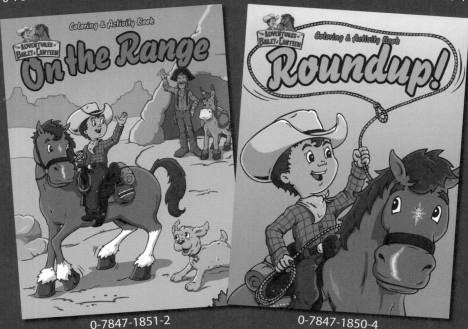

0-7847-1851-2

0-7847-1850-4